Share your completed journal pages
on instagram @mtlottbooks
#fartjournal

Sign up for email list
www.MTLottBooks.com

Connect with M.T. Lott on facebook
www.facebook.com/authormtlott

BOOKS BY M.T. LOTT

 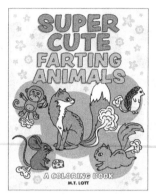 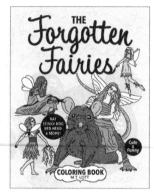

 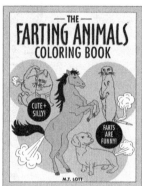

Available for purchase at your favorite on-line bookstore.
Check out sample pages at the back of this book!

Copyright © 2018 by MT Lott
www.mtlottbooks.com

ISBN: 9781726800907

No part of this publication may be reproduced, distributed or transmitted in any form or by any means, without the prior written permission of the publisher, except in the case of brief quotations embodied in critical reviews and certain other noncommerical uses permitted by copyright law.

FART

DATE: _____
TIME: _____
LOCATION: _____

Did it smell?
☐ Yes ☐ No

IF YES, CHECK ALL THAT APPLY
- ☐ cheesy
- ☐ beany
- ☐ eggy
- ☐ oniony
- ☐ malty
- ☐ musty
- ☐ nutty
- ☐ skunky
- ☐ sulfur
- ☐ spicy
- ☐ pungent
- ☐ earthy
- ☐ prune
- ☐ cabbage
- ☐ funk
- ☐ taco

Smell-O-meter
(fill in the boxes)

not too bad ⟹ eye-watering

DID YOU TAKE OWNERSHIP? ☐ Yes ☐ No
☐ Blamed dog

fill in to appropriate level

- ninja
- quack
- blast
- engine
- nuclear

NOISE LEVEL

Any witnesses? ☐ Yes ☐ No

IF YES, who? _____
REACTION? _____

DRAW YOUR FART ←

OTHER NOTES: _____

FART

DATE: _____
TIME: _____
LOCATION: _____

Did it smell?
☐ Yes ☐ No

IF YES, CHECK ALL THAT APPLY
- ☐ cheesy
- ☐ beany
- ☐ eggy
- ☐ oniony
- ☐ malty
- ☐ musty
- ☐ nutty
- ☐ skunky
- ☐ sulfur
- ☐ spicy
- ☐ pungent
- ☐ earthy
- ☐ prune
- ☐ cabbage
- ☐ funk
- ☐ taco

Smell-O-meter
(fill in the boxes)

not too bad ⟹ eye-watering

DID YOU TAKE OWNERSHIP? ☐ Yes ☐ No
☐ Blamed dog

fill in to appropriate level — ninja, quack, blast, engine, nuclear

NOISE LEVEL

Any witnesses? ☐ Yes ☐ No
If YES, who? _____
REACTION? _____

DRAW YOUR FART ←

OTHER NOTES: _____

FART

DATE:
TIME:
LOCATION:

Did it smell?
☐ Yes ☐ No

Smell-O-meter
(fill in the boxes)

not too bad ⟶ eye-watering

IF YES, CHECK ALL THAT APPLY

☐ cheesy
☐ beany
☐ eggy
☐ oniony
☐ malty
☐ musty
☐ nutty
☐ skunky
☐ sulfur
☐ spicy
☐ pungent
☐ earthy
☐ prune
☐ cabbage
☐ funk
☐ taco

DID YOU TAKE OWNERSHIP? ☐ Yes ☐ No
☐ Blamed dog

fill in to appropriate level

- ninja
- quack
- blast
- engine
- nuclear

NOISE LEVEL

Any witnesses?
☐ Yes ☐ No

If YES, who?
REACTION?

DRAW YOUR FART ←

OTHER NOTES:

FART

DATE:
TIME:
LOCATION:

Did it smell?
☐ Yes ☐ No

Smell-O-meter
(fill in the boxes)

not too bad ⟹ eye-watering

IF YES, CHECK ALL THAT APPLY
- ☐ cheesy
- ☐ beany
- ☐ eggy
- ☐ oniony
- ☐ malty
- ☐ musty
- ☐ nutty
- ☐ skunky
- ☐ sulfur
- ☐ spicy
- ☐ pungent
- ☐ earthy
- ☐ prune
- ☐ cabbage
- ☐ funk
- ☐ taco

DID YOU TAKE OWNERSHIP? ☐ Yes ☐ No ☐ Blamed dog

fill in to appropriate level

- quack
- blast
- engine
- ninja
- nuclear

NOISE LEVEL

Any witnesses? ☐ Yes ☐ No

If YES, who?
REACTION?

DRAW YOUR FART ←

OTHER NOTES:

FART

DATE: _____
TIME: _____
LOCATION: _____

Did it smell?
☐ Yes ☐ No

IF YES, CHECK ALL THAT APPLY
- ☐ cheesy
- ☐ beany
- ☐ eggy
- ☐ oniony
- ☐ malty
- ☐ musty
- ☐ nutty
- ☐ skunky
- ☐ sulfur
- ☐ spicy
- ☐ pungent
- ☐ earthy
- ☐ prune
- ☐ cabbage
- ☐ funk
- ☐ taco

Smell-O-meter
(fill in the boxes)

not too bad ⟹ eye-watering

DID YOU TAKE OWNERSHIP? ☐ Yes ☐ No
☐ Blamed dog

NOISE LEVEL
fill in to appropriate level

- ninja
- quack
- blast
- engine
- nuclear

Any witnesses?
☐ Yes ☐ No

IF YES, who? _____
REACTION? _____

DRAW YOUR FART ←

OTHER NOTES: _____

FART

DATE:
TIME:
LOCATION:

Did it smell?
☐ Yes ☐ No

IF YES, CHECK ALL THAT APPLY
- ☐ cheesy
- ☐ beany
- ☐ eggy
- ☐ oniony
- ☐ malty
- ☐ musty
- ☐ nutty
- ☐ skunky
- ☐ sulfur
- ☐ spicy
- ☐ pungent
- ☐ earthy
- ☐ prune
- ☐ cabbage
- ☐ funk
- ☐ taco

Smell-O-meter
(fill in the boxes)

not too bad ⟶ eye-watering

DID YOU TAKE OWNERSHIP? ☐ Yes ☐ No
☐ Blamed dog

fill in to appropriate level

- quack
- blast
- engine
- ninja
- nuclear

NOISE LEVEL

Any witnesses? ☐ Yes ☐ No

If YES, who?
REACTION?

DRAW YOUR FART ←

OTHER NOTES:

FART

DATE:
TIME:
LOCATION:

Did it smell?
☐ Yes ☐ No

Smell-O-meter
(fill in the boxes)

not too bad ⇒ eye-watering

IF YES, CHECK ALL THAT APPLY
- ☐ cheesy
- ☐ beany
- ☐ eggy
- ☐ oniony
- ☐ malty
- ☐ musty
- ☐ nutty
- ☐ skunky
- ☐ sulfur
- ☐ spicy
- ☐ pungent
- ☐ earthy
- ☐ prune
- ☐ cabbage
- ☐ funk
- ☐ taco

DID YOU TAKE OWNERSHIP? ☐ Yes ☐ No
☐ Blamed dog

fill in to appropriate level

- quack
- blast
- engine
- ninja
- nuclear

NOISE LEVEL

Any witnesses? ☐ Yes ☐ No
If YES, who?
REACTION?

DRAW YOUR FART ←

OTHER NOTES:

FART

DATE: _____
TIME: _____
LOCATION: _____

Did it smell?
☐ Yes ☐ No

Smell-O-meter
(fill in the boxes)

not too bad ⟹ eye-watering

IF YES, CHECK ALL THAT APPLY
- ☐ cheesy
- ☐ beany
- ☐ eggy
- ☐ oniony
- ☐ malty
- ☐ musty
- ☐ nutty
- ☐ skunky
- ☐ sulfur
- ☐ spicy
- ☐ pungent
- ☐ earthy
- ☐ prune
- ☐ cabbage
- ☐ funk
- ☐ taco

DID YOU TAKE OWNERSHIP? ☐ Yes ☐ No
☐ Blamed dog

NOISE LEVEL
fill in to appropriate level
- ninja
- quack
- blast
- engine
- nuclear

Any witnesses? ☐ Yes ☐ No
IF YES, who? _____
REACTION? _____

DRAW YOUR FART ←

OTHER NOTES: _____

FART

DATE: _____
TIME: _____
LOCATION: _____

Did it smell?
☐ Yes ☐ No

IF YES, CHECK ALL THAT APPLY
- ☐ cheesy
- ☐ beany
- ☐ eggy
- ☐ oniony
- ☐ malty
- ☐ musty
- ☐ nutty
- ☐ skunky
- ☐ sulfur
- ☐ spicy
- ☐ pungent
- ☐ earthy
- ☐ prune
- ☐ cabbage
- ☐ funk
- ☐ taco

Smell-O-meter
(fill in the boxes)

not too bad ⟹ eye-watering

DID YOU TAKE OWNERSHIP? ☐ Yes ☐ No
☐ Blamed dog

NOISE LEVEL
(fill in to appropriate level)
- ninja
- quack
- blast
- engine
- nuclear

Any witnesses? ☐ Yes ☐ No
If YES, who? _____
REACTION? _____

DRAW YOUR FART ⬅

OTHER NOTES: _____

FART

DATE: _____
TIME: _____
LOCATION: _____

Did it smell?
☐ Yes ☐ No

IF YES, CHECK ALL THAT APPLY
- ☐ cheesy
- ☐ beany
- ☐ eggy
- ☐ oniony
- ☐ malty
- ☐ musty
- ☐ nutty
- ☐ skunky
- ☐ sulfur
- ☐ spicy
- ☐ pungent
- ☐ earthy
- ☐ prune
- ☐ cabbage
- ☐ funk
- ☐ taco

Smell-O-meter
(fill in the boxes)

not too bad ➡ eye-watering

DID YOU TAKE OWNERSHIP? ☐ Yes ☐ No ☐ Blamed dog

fill in to appropriate level

- ninja
- quack
- blast
- engine
- nuclear

NOISE LEVEL

Any witnesses? ☐ Yes ☐ No

If YES, who? _____
REACTION? _____

DRAW YOUR FART ←

OTHER NOTES: _____

FART # ◯

DATE: _____ **TIME:** _____ **LOCATION:** _____

Did it smell?
☐ Yes ☐ No

IF YES, CHECK ALL THAT APPLY
- ☐ cheesy
- ☐ beany
- ☐ eggy
- ☐ oniony
- ☐ malty
- ☐ musty
- ☐ nutty
- ☐ skunky
- ☐ sulfur
- ☐ spicy
- ☐ pungent
- ☐ earthy
- ☐ prune
- ☐ cabbage
- ☐ funk
- ☐ taco

Smell-O-meter
(fill in the boxes)

[ ][ ][ ][ ][ ][ ][ ][ ][ ][ ][ ][ ][ ][ ][ ]

not too bad ⟹ eye-watering

DID YOU TAKE OWNERSHIP? ☐ Yes ☐ No ☐ Blamed dog

fill in to appropriate level

Noise level options: quack | blast | engine | ninja | nuclear

NOISE LEVEL

Any witnesses? ■ Yes ■ No

If YES, who? _____
REACTION? _____

DRAW YOUR FART ←

OTHER NOTES: _____

FART

DATE:
TIME:
LOCATION:

Did it smell?
☐ Yes ☐ No

Smell-O-meter
(fill in the boxes)

not too bad ⟶ eye-watering

IF YES, CHECK ALL THAT APPLY
- ☐ cheesy
- ☐ beany
- ☐ eggy
- ☐ oniony
- ☐ malty
- ☐ musty
- ☐ nutty
- ☐ skunky
- ☐ sulfur
- ☐ spicy
- ☐ pungent
- ☐ earthy
- ☐ prune
- ☐ cabbage
- ☐ funk
- ☐ taco

DID YOU TAKE OWNERSHIP? ☐ Yes ☐ No
☐ Blamed dog

fill in to appropriate level
- ninja
- quack
- blast
- engine
- nuclear

NOISE LEVEL

Any witnesses?
■ Yes ■ No

If YES, who?
REACTION?

DRAW YOUR FART ⬅

OTHER NOTES:

FART

DATE: _____
TIME: _____
LOCATION: _____

Did it smell?
☐ Yes ☐ No

Smell-O-meter
(fill in the boxes)

[ ][ ][ ][ ][ ][ ][ ][ ][ ][ ][ ][ ][ ][ ][ ][ ][ ]

not too bad ⟹ eye-watering

IF YES, CHECK ALL THAT APPLY
- ☐ cheesy
- ☐ beany
- ☐ eggy
- ☐ oniony
- ☐ malty
- ☐ musty
- ☐ nutty
- ☐ skunky
- ☐ sulfur
- ☐ spicy
- ☐ pungent
- ☐ earthy
- ☐ prune
- ☐ cabbage
- ☐ funk
- ☐ taco

DID YOU TAKE OWNERSHIP? ☐ Yes ☐ No
☐ Blamed dog

NOISE LEVEL
fill in to appropriate level
- ninja
- quack
- blast
- engine
- nuclear

Any witnesses?
☐ Yes ☐ No

If YES, who? _____
REACTION? _____

DRAW YOUR FART ←

OTHER NOTES: _____

FART

DATE: _____
TIME: _____
LOCATION: _____

Did it smell?
☐ Yes ☐ No

IF YES, CHECK ALL THAT APPLY
- ☐ cheesy
- ☐ beany
- ☐ eggy
- ☐ oniony
- ☐ malty
- ☐ musty
- ☐ nutty
- ☐ skunky
- ☐ sulfur
- ☐ spicy
- ☐ pungent
- ☐ earthy
- ☐ prune
- ☐ cabbage
- ☐ funk
- ☐ taco

Smell-O-meter
(fill in the boxes)

not too bad ➡ eye-watering

DID YOU TAKE OWNERSHIP? ☐ Yes ☐ No ☐ Blamed dog

NOISE LEVEL
fill in to appropriate level

- ninja
- quack
- blast
- engine
- nuclear

Any witnesses? ☐ Yes ☐ No

IF YES, who? _____
REACTION? _____

DRAW YOUR FART ←

OTHER NOTES: _____

FART #　　　　　LOCATION:

DATE:　　　　TIME:

Did it smell?
☐ Yes ☐ No

Smell-O-meter
(fill in the boxes)

not too bad ➡ eye-watering

IF YES, CHECK ALL THAT APPLY

- ☐ cheesy
- ☐ beany
- ☐ eggy
- ☐ oniony
- ☐ malty
- ☐ musty
- ☐ nutty
- ☐ skunky
- ☐ sulfur
- ☐ spicy
- ☐ pungent
- ☐ earthy
- ☐ prune
- ☐ cabbage
- ☐ funk
- ☐ taco

DID YOU TAKE OWNERSHIP? ☐ Yes ☐ No ☐ Blamed dog

fill in to appropriate level

- quack
- blast
- engine
- ninja
- nuclear

NOISE LEVEL

Any witnesses?
☐ Yes ☐ No

If YES, who? _____
REACTION? _____

DRAW YOUR FART ←

OTHER NOTES: _____

FART # ◯

DATE: _____
TIME: _____
LOCATION: _____

Did it smell?
☐ Yes ☐ No

Smell-O-meter
(fill in the boxes)

☐☐☐☐☐☐☐☐☐☐☐☐☐

not too bad ⟹ eye-watering

IF YES, CHECK ALL THAT APPLY
- ☐ cheesy
- ☐ beany
- ☐ eggy
- ☐ oniony
- ☐ malty
- ☐ musty
- ☐ nutty
- ☐ skunky
- ☐ sulfur
- ☐ spicy
- ☐ pungent
- ☐ earthy
- ☐ prune
- ☐ cabbage
- ☐ funk
- ☐ taco

DID YOU TAKE OWNERSHIP? ☐ Yes ☐ No ☐ Blamed dog

fill in to appropriate level

- quack
- blast
- engine
- ninja
- nuclear

NOISE LEVEL

Any witnesses? ☐ Yes ☐ No

If YES, who? _____
REACTION? _____

DRAW YOUR FART ←

OTHER NOTES: _____

FART # ____

DATE: _____ **TIME:** _____ **LOCATION:** _____

Did it smell?
☐ Yes ☐ No

IF YES, CHECK ALL THAT APPLY
- ☐ cheesy
- ☐ beany
- ☐ eggy
- ☐ oniony
- ☐ malty
- ☐ musty
- ☐ nutty
- ☐ skunky
- ☐ sulfur
- ☐ spicy
- ☐ pungent
- ☐ earthy
- ☐ prune
- ☐ cabbage
- ☐ funk
- ☐ taco

Smell-O-meter
(fill in the boxes)

not too bad ⇨ eye-watering

DID YOU TAKE OWNERSHIP? ☐ Yes ☐ No ☐ Blamed dog

NOISE LEVEL
fill in to appropriate level
- ninja
- quack
- blast
- engine
- nuclear

Any witnesses? ☐ Yes ☐ No

If YES, who? _____
REACTION? _____

DRAW YOUR FART ←

OTHER NOTES: _____

FART

DATE: _____
TIME: _____
LOCATION: _____

Did it smell?
☐ Yes ☐ No

IF YES, CHECK ALL THAT APPLY
- ☐ cheesy
- ☐ beany
- ☐ eggy
- ☐ oniony
- ☐ malty
- ☐ musty
- ☐ nutty
- ☐ skunky
- ☐ sulfur
- ☐ spicy
- ☐ pungent
- ☐ earthy
- ☐ prune
- ☐ cabbage
- ☐ funk
- ☐ taco

Smell-O-meter
(fill in the boxes)

not too bad ➡ eye-watering

DID YOU TAKE OWNERSHIP? ☐ Yes ☐ No
☐ Blamed dog

NOISE LEVEL
fill in to appropriate level
- ninja
- quack
- blast
- engine
- nuclear

Any witnesses?
☐ Yes ☐ No

IF YES, who? _____
REACTION? _____

DRAW YOUR FART ⬅

OTHER NOTES: _____

FART

DATE: _____
TIME: _____
LOCATION: _____

Did it smell?
☐ Yes ☐ No

Smell-O-meter
(fill in the boxes)

not too bad ⟹ eye-watering

IF YES, CHECK ALL THAT APPLY
- ☐ cheesy
- ☐ beany
- ☐ eggy
- ☐ oniony
- ☐ malty
- ☐ musty
- ☐ nutty
- ☐ skunky
- ☐ sulfur
- ☐ spicy
- ☐ pungent
- ☐ earthy
- ☐ prune
- ☐ cabbage
- ☐ funk
- ☐ taco

DID YOU TAKE OWNERSHIP? ☐ Yes ☐ No
☐ Blamed dog

NOISE LEVEL
fill in to appropriate level
- ninja
- quack
- blast
- engine
- nuclear

Any witnesses? ☐ Yes ☐ No
IF YES, who? _____
REACTION? _____

DRAW YOUR FART ←

OTHER NOTES: _____

FART # ◯

DATE: _____
TIME: _____
LOCATION: _____

Did it smell?
☐ Yes ☐ No

Smell-O-meter
(fill in the boxes)

[□□□□□□□□□□□□□□]

not too bad ➡ eye-watering

IF YES, CHECK ALL THAT APPLY
- ☐ cheesy
- ☐ beany
- ☐ eggy
- ☐ oniony
- ☐ malty
- ☐ musty
- ☐ nutty
- ☐ skunky
- ☐ sulfur
- ☐ spicy
- ☐ pungent
- ☐ earthy
- ☐ prune
- ☐ cabbage
- ☐ funk
- ☐ taco

DID YOU TAKE OWNERSHIP? ☐ Yes ☐ No
☐ Blamed dog

fill in to appropriate level

- ninja
- quack
- blast
- engine
- nuclear

NOISE LEVEL

Any witnesses? ☐ Yes ☐ No

If YES, who? _____
REACTION? _____

DRAW YOUR FART ←

OTHER NOTES: _____

FART

DATE: _____
TIME: _____
LOCATION: _____

Did it smell?
☐ Yes ☐ No

Smell-O-meter
(fill in the boxes)

not too bad ⟹ eye-watering

IF YES, CHECK ALL THAT APPLY
- ☐ cheesy
- ☐ beany
- ☐ eggy
- ☐ oniony
- ☐ malty
- ☐ musty
- ☐ nutty
- ☐ skunky
- ☐ sulfur
- ☐ spicy
- ☐ pungent
- ☐ earthy
- ☐ prune
- ☐ cabbage
- ☐ funk
- ☐ taco

DID YOU TAKE OWNERSHIP? ☐ Yes ☐ No ☐ Blamed dog

fill in to appropriate level

- ninja
- quack
- blast
- engine
- nuclear

NOISE LEVEL

Any witnesses? ☐ Yes ☐ No

If YES, who? _____
REACTION? _____

DRAW YOUR FART ←

OTHER NOTES: _____

FART

DATE: _____
TIME: _____
LOCATION: _____

Did it smell?
☐ Yes ☐ No

IF YES, CHECK ALL THAT APPLY
- ☐ cheesy
- ☐ beany
- ☐ eggy
- ☐ oniony
- ☐ malty
- ☐ musty
- ☐ nutty
- ☐ skunky
- ☐ sulfur
- ☐ spicy
- ☐ pungent
- ☐ earthy
- ☐ prune
- ☐ cabbage
- ☐ funk
- ☐ taco

Smell-O-meter
(fill in the boxes)

not too bad ➡ eye-watering

DID YOU TAKE OWNERSHIP? ☐ Yes ☐ No
☐ Blamed dog

fill in to appropriate level

- ninja
- quack
- blast
- engine
- nuclear

NOISE LEVEL

Any witnesses? ☐ Yes ☐ No

If YES, who? _____
REACTION? _____

DRAW YOUR FART ←

OTHER NOTES: _____

FART

DATE: _____
TIME: _____
LOCATION: _____

Did it smell?
☐ Yes ☐ No

Smell-O-meter
(fill in the boxes)

not too bad ⟹ eye-watering

IF YES, CHECK ALL THAT APPLY
- ☐ cheesy
- ☐ beany
- ☐ eggy
- ☐ oniony
- ☐ malty
- ☐ musty
- ☐ nutty
- ☐ skunky
- ☐ sulfur
- ☐ spicy
- ☐ pungent
- ☐ earthy
- ☐ prune
- ☐ cabbage
- ☐ funk
- ☐ taco

DID YOU TAKE OWNERSHIP?
☐ Yes ☐ No
☐ Blamed dog

fill in to appropriate level

- ninja
- quack
- blast
- engine
- nuclear

NOISE LEVEL

Any witnesses?
☐ Yes ☐ No

IF YES, who? _____
REACTION? _____

DRAW YOUR FART ←

OTHER NOTES: _____

FART

DATE: _____
TIME: _____
LOCATION: _____

Did it smell?
☐ Yes ☐ No

Smell-O-meter
(fill in the boxes)

[ ][ ][ ][ ][ ][ ][ ][ ][ ][ ][ ][ ][ ][ ][ ]

not too bad ⟹ eye-watering

DID YOU TAKE OWNERSHIP? ☐ Yes ☐ No
☐ Blamed dog

IF YES, CHECK ALL THAT APPLY
- ☐ cheesy
- ☐ beany
- ☐ eggy
- ☐ oniony
- ☐ malty
- ☐ musty
- ☐ nutty
- ☐ skunky
- ☐ sulfur
- ☐ spicy
- ☐ pungent
- ☐ earthy
- ☐ prune
- ☐ cabbage
- ☐ funk
- ☐ taco

NOISE LEVEL
fill in to appropriate level

- ninja
- quack
- blast
- engine
- nuclear

Any witnesses?
☐ Yes ☐ No

If YES, who? _____
REACTION? _____

DRAW YOUR FART ←

OTHER NOTES: _____

FART #: ____

DATE: ____
TIME: ____
LOCATION: ____

Did it smell?
- ☐ Yes
- ☐ No

IF YES, CHECK ALL THAT APPLY
- ☐ cheesy
- ☐ beany
- ☐ eggy
- ☐ oniony
- ☐ malty
- ☐ musty
- ☐ nutty
- ☐ skunky
- ☐ sulfur
- ☐ spicy
- ☐ pungent
- ☐ earthy
- ☐ prune
- ☐ cabbage
- ☐ funk
- ☐ taco

Smell-O-meter
(fill in the boxes)

not too bad ⇒ eye-watering

DID YOU TAKE OWNERSHIP? ☐ Yes ☐ No ☐ Blamed dog

NOISE LEVEL
fill in to appropriate level
- ninja
- quack
- blast
- engine
- nuclear

Any witnesses? ☐ Yes ☐ No
If yes, who? ____
REACTION? ____

DRAW YOUR FART ←

OTHER NOTES: ____

FART

DATE: _____
TIME: _____
LOCATION: _____

Did it smell?
☐ Yes ☐ No

IF YES, CHECK ALL THAT APPLY
- ☐ cheesy
- ☐ beany
- ☐ eggy
- ☐ oniony
- ☐ malty
- ☐ musty
- ☐ nutty
- ☐ skunky
- ☐ sulfur
- ☐ spicy
- ☐ pungent
- ☐ earthy
- ☐ prune
- ☐ cabbage
- ☐ funk
- ☐ taco

Smell-O-meter
(fill in the boxes)

not too bad ➡ eye-watering

DID YOU TAKE OWNERSHIP? ☐ Yes ☐ No ☐ Blamed dog

fill in to appropriate level

- quack
- blast
- engine
- ninja
- nuclear

NOISE LEVEL

Any witnesses? ☐ Yes ☐ No

If yes, who? _____
REACTION? _____

DRAW YOUR FART ⬅

OTHER NOTES: _____

FART # ___

DATE: ___
TIME: ___
LOCATION: ___

Did it smell? ☐ Yes ☐ No

Smell-O-meter
(fill in the boxes)

☐☐☐☐☐☐☐☐☐☐☐☐

not too bad ⟹ eye-watering

IF YES, CHECK ALL THAT APPLY
- ☐ cheesy
- ☐ beany
- ☐ eggy
- ☐ oniony
- ☐ malty
- ☐ musty
- ☐ nutty
- ☐ skunky
- ☐ sulfur
- ☐ spicy
- ☐ pungent
- ☐ earthy
- ☐ prune
- ☐ cabbage
- ☐ funk
- ☐ taco

DID YOU TAKE OWNERSHIP? ☐ Yes ☐ No ☐ Blamed dog

fill in to appropriate level

- ninja
- quack
- blast
- engine
- nuclear

NOISE LEVEL

Any witnesses? ☐ Yes ☐ No

If YES, who? ___
REACTION? ___

DRAW YOUR FART ←

OTHER NOTES: ___

FART

DATE:
TIME:
LOCATION:

Did it smell?
☐ Yes ☐ No

Smell-O-meter
(fill in the boxes)

not too bad ⟶ eye-watering

IF YES, CHECK ALL THAT APPLY
- ☐ cheesy
- ☐ beany
- ☐ eggy
- ☐ oniony
- ☐ malty
- ☐ musty
- ☐ nutty
- ☐ skunky
- ☐ sulfur
- ☐ spicy
- ☐ pungent
- ☐ earthy
- ☐ prune
- ☐ cabbage
- ☐ funk
- ☐ taco

DID YOU TAKE OWNERSHIP? ☐ Yes ☐ No ☐ Blamed dog

fill in to appropriate level

quack | blast | engine
ninja | | nuclear

NOISE LEVEL

Any witnesses? ☐ Yes ☐ No

If YES, who?
REACTION?

DRAW YOUR FART ←

OTHER NOTES:

FART

DATE: _____
TIME: _____
LOCATION: _____

Did it smell?
☐ Yes ☐ No

Smell-O-meter
(fill in the boxes)

not too bad ⟹ eye-watering

IF YES, CHECK ALL THAT APPLY
- ☐ cheesy
- ☐ beany
- ☐ eggy
- ☐ oniony
- ☐ malty
- ☐ musty
- ☐ nutty
- ☐ skunky
- ☐ sulfur
- ☐ spicy
- ☐ pungent
- ☐ earthy
- ☐ prune
- ☐ cabbage
- ☐ funk
- ☐ taco

DID YOU TAKE OWNERSHIP? ☐ Yes ☐ No
☐ Blamed dog

NOISE LEVEL
fill in to appropriate level
- quack
- blast
- engine
- ninja
- nuclear

Any witnesses?
☐ Yes ☐ No

If YES, who? _____
REACTION? _____

DRAW YOUR FART ←

OTHER NOTES: _____

FART

DATE: _____
TIME: _____
LOCATION: _____

Did it smell?
☐ Yes ☐ No

IF YES, CHECK ALL THAT APPLY
- ☐ cheesy
- ☐ beany
- ☐ eggy
- ☐ oniony
- ☐ malty
- ☐ musty
- ☐ nutty
- ☐ skunky
- ☐ sulfur
- ☐ spicy
- ☐ pungent
- ☐ earthy
- ☐ prune
- ☐ cabbage
- ☐ funk
- ☐ taco

Smell-O-meter
(fill in the boxes)

not too bad ➡ eye-watering

DID YOU TAKE OWNERSHIP? ☐ Yes ☐ No ☐ Blamed dog

fill in to appropriate level

- quack
- blast
- engine
- ninja
- nuclear

NOISE LEVEL

Any witnesses? ☐ Yes ☐ No

If YES, who? _____
REACTION? _____

DRAW YOUR FART ←

OTHER NOTES: _____

FART # ◯

DATE: _____

TIME: _____

LOCATION: _____

Did it smell?
☐ Yes ☐ No

Smell-O-meter
(fill in the boxes)

[ ][ ][ ][ ][ ][ ][ ][ ][ ][ ][ ][ ][ ]

not too bad ⟹ eye-watering

IF YES, CHECK ALL THAT APPLY
- ☐ cheesy
- ☐ beany
- ☐ eggy
- ☐ oniony
- ☐ malty
- ☐ musty
- ☐ nutty
- ☐ skunky
- ☐ sulfur
- ☐ spicy
- ☐ pungent
- ☐ earthy
- ☐ prune
- ☐ cabbage
- ☐ funk
- ☐ taco

DID YOU TAKE OWNERSHIP? ☐ Yes ☐ No ☐ Blamed dog

fill in to appropriate level

Noise level: ninja / quack / blast / engine / nuclear

NOISE LEVEL

Any witnesses? ☐ Yes ☐ No

If YES, who? _____

REACTION? _____

DRAW YOUR FART ←

OTHER NOTES: _____

FART

DATE: ....
TIME: ....
LOCATION: ....

Did it smell?
☐ Yes ☐ No

IF YES, CHECK ALL THAT APPLY
- ☐ cheesy
- ☐ beany
- ☐ eggy
- ☐ oniony
- ☐ malty
- ☐ musty
- ☐ nutty
- ☐ skunky
- ☐ sulfur
- ☐ spicy
- ☐ pungent
- ☐ earthy
- ☐ prune
- ☐ cabbage
- ☐ funk
- ☐ taco

Smell-O-meter
(fill in the boxes)

not too bad ⟹ eye-watering

DID YOU TAKE OWNERSHIP? ☐ Yes ☐ No ☐ Blamed dog

fill in to appropriate level

ninja | quack | blast | engine | nuclear

NOISE LEVEL

Any witnesses? ■ Yes ■ No
If yes, who? ....
REACTION? ....

DRAW YOUR FART ←

OTHER NOTES: ....

FART

DATE: _____
TIME: _____
LOCATION: _____

Did it smell?
☐ Yes ☐ No

Smell-O-meter
(fill in the boxes)

☐☐☐☐☐☐☐☐☐☐

not too bad ⟹ eye-watering

IF YES, CHECK ALL THAT APPLY

☐ cheesy
☐ beany
☐ eggy
☐ oniony
☐ malty
☐ musty
☐ nutty
☐ skunky
☐ sulfur
☐ spicy
☐ pungent
☐ earthy
☐ prune
☐ cabbage
☐ funk
☐ taco

DID YOU TAKE OWNERSHIP? ☐ Yes ☐ No ☐ Blamed dog

fill in to appropriate level

- quack
- blast
- engine
- ninja
- nuclear

NOISE LEVEL

Any witnesses?
☐ Yes ☐ No

If YES, who? _____
REACTION? _____

DRAW YOUR FART ←

OTHER NOTES: _____

FART

DATE: _____
TIME: _____
LOCATION: _____

Did it smell?
☐ Yes ☐ No

IF YES, CHECK ALL THAT APPLY
- ☐ cheesy
- ☐ beany
- ☐ eggy
- ☐ oniony
- ☐ malty
- ☐ musty
- ☐ nutty
- ☐ skunky
- ☐ sulfur
- ☐ spicy
- ☐ pungent
- ☐ earthy
- ☐ prune
- ☐ cabbage
- ☐ funk
- ☐ taco

Smell-O-meter
(fill in the boxes)

not too bad ⟹ eye-watering

DID YOU TAKE OWNERSHIP? ☐ Yes ☐ No ☐ Blamed dog

fill in to appropriate level

- ninja
- quack
- blast
- engine
- nuclear

NOISE LEVEL

Any witnesses? ☐ Yes ☐ No
If YES, who? _____
REACTION? _____

DRAW YOUR FART ←

OTHER NOTES: _____

FART # ◯

DATE: _____
TIME: _____
LOCATION: _____

Did it smell?
☐ Yes ☐ No

Smell-O-meter
(fill in the boxes)

not too bad ⟹ eye-watering

IF YES, CHECK ALL THAT APPLY
- ☐ cheesy
- ☐ beany
- ☐ eggy
- ☐ oniony
- ☐ malty
- ☐ musty
- ☐ nutty
- ☐ skunky
- ☐ sulfur
- ☐ spicy
- ☐ pungent
- ☐ earthy
- ☐ prune
- ☐ cabbage
- ☐ funk
- ☐ taco

DID YOU TAKE OWNERSHIP? ☐ Yes ☐ No ☐ Blamed dog

fill in to appropriate level

- quack
- blast
- engine
- ninja
- nuclear

NOISE LEVEL

Any witnesses? ☐ Yes ☐ No
If YES, who? _____
REACTION? _____

DRAW YOUR FART ←

OTHER NOTES: _____

FART

DATE: _____
TIME: _____
LOCATION: _____

Did it smell?
☐ Yes ☐ No

Smell-O-meter
(fill in the boxes)

not too bad ⟹ eye-watering

DID YOU TAKE OWNERSHIP? ☐ Yes ☐ No
☐ Blamed dog

IF YES, CHECK ALL THAT APPLY
- ☐ cheesy
- ☐ beany
- ☐ eggy
- ☐ oniony
- ☐ malty
- ☐ musty
- ☐ nutty
- ☐ skunky
- ☐ sulfur
- ☐ spicy
- ☐ pungent
- ☐ earthy
- ☐ prune
- ☐ cabbage
- ☐ funk
- ☐ taco

NOISE LEVEL
fill in to appropriate level
- ninja
- quack
- blast
- engine
- nuclear

Any witnesses?
☐ Yes ☐ No

If YES, who? _____
REACTION? _____

DRAW YOUR FART ←

OTHER NOTES: _____

FART # ___

DATE: ___
TIME: ___
LOCATION: ___

Did it smell?
☐ Yes ☐ No

IF YES, CHECK ALL THAT APPLY
- ☐ cheesy
- ☐ beany
- ☐ eggy
- ☐ oniony
- ☐ malty
- ☐ musty
- ☐ nutty
- ☐ skunky
- ☐ sulfur
- ☐ spicy
- ☐ pungent
- ☐ earthy
- ☐ prune
- ☐ cabbage
- ☐ funk
- ☐ taco

Smell-O-meter
(fill in the boxes)

not too bad ⟹ eye-watering

DID YOU TAKE OWNERSHIP? ☐ Yes ☐ No
☐ Blamed dog

NOISE LEVEL
fill in to appropriate level

- ninja
- quack
- blast
- engine
- nuclear

Any witnesses?
☐ Yes ☐ No

IF YES, who? ___
REACTION? ___

DRAW YOUR FART ←

OTHER NOTES: ___

FART

DATE: _____
TIME: _____
LOCATION: _____

Did it smell?
☐ Yes ☐ No

IF YES, CHECK ALL THAT APPLY
- ☐ cheesy
- ☐ beany
- ☐ eggy
- ☐ oniony
- ☐ malty
- ☐ musty
- ☐ nutty
- ☐ skunky
- ☐ sulfur
- ☐ spicy
- ☐ pungent
- ☐ earthy
- ☐ prune
- ☐ cabbage
- ☐ funk
- ☐ taco

Smell-O-meter
(fill in the boxes)

not too bad ➡ eye-watering

DID YOU TAKE OWNERSHIP? ☐ Yes ☐ No
☐ Blamed dog

NOISE LEVEL
fill in to appropriate level
- ninja
- quack
- blast
- engine
- nuclear

Any witnesses? ☐ Yes ☐ No

If yes, who? _____
REACTION? _____

DRAW YOUR FART ⬅

OTHER NOTES: _____

FART # ◯

DATE: _____

TIME: _____

LOCATION: _____

Did it smell?
☐ Yes ☐ No

IF YES, CHECK ALL THAT APPLY
- ☐ cheesy
- ☐ beany
- ☐ eggy
- ☐ oniony
- ☐ malty
- ☐ musty
- ☐ nutty
- ☐ skunky
- ☐ sulfur
- ☐ spicy
- ☐ pungent
- ☐ earthy
- ☐ prune
- ☐ cabbage
- ☐ funk
- ☐ taco

Smell-O-meter
(fill in the boxes)

not too bad ⟹ eye-watering

DID YOU TAKE OWNERSHIP? ☐ Yes ☐ No
☐ Blamed dog

fill in to appropriate level

NOISE LEVEL
- ninja
- quack
- blast
- engine
- nuclear

Any witnesses?
☐ Yes ☐ No

If YES, who? _____

REACTION? _____

DRAW YOUR FART ←

OTHER NOTES: _____

FART

DATE: _____
TIME: _____
LOCATION: _____

Did it smell?
☐ Yes ☐ No

Smell-O-meter
(fill in the boxes)

not too bad ➡ eye-watering

IF YES, CHECK ALL THAT APPLY
- ☐ cheesy
- ☐ beany
- ☐ eggy
- ☐ oniony
- ☐ malty
- ☐ musty
- ☐ nutty
- ☐ skunky
- ☐ sulfur
- ☐ spicy
- ☐ pungent
- ☐ earthy
- ☐ prune
- ☐ cabbage
- ☐ funk
- ☐ taco

DID YOU TAKE OWNERSHIP? ☐ Yes ☐ No
☐ Blamed dog

fill in to appropriate level

quack | blast | engine
ninja | | nuclear

NOISE LEVEL

Any witnesses? ☐ Yes ☐ No
If YES, who? _____
REACTION? _____

DRAW YOUR FART ⬅

OTHER NOTES: _____

FART

DATE: _____
TIME: _____
LOCATION: _____

Did it smell?
☐ Yes ☐ No

IF YES, CHECK ALL THAT APPLY
- ☐ cheesy
- ☐ beany
- ☐ eggy
- ☐ oniony
- ☐ malty
- ☐ musty
- ☐ nutty
- ☐ skunky
- ☐ sulfur
- ☐ spicy
- ☐ pungent
- ☐ earthy
- ☐ prune
- ☐ cabbage
- ☐ funk
- ☐ taco

Smell-O-meter
(fill in the boxes)

not too bad ➔ eye-watering

DID YOU TAKE OWNERSHIP? ☐ Yes ☐ No
☐ Blamed dog

NOISE LEVEL
fill in to appropriate level
- ninja
- quack
- blast
- engine
- nuclear

Any witnesses? ☐ Yes ☐ No
If YES, who? _____
REACTION? _____

DRAW YOUR FART ←

OTHER NOTES: _____

FART

DATE: _____
TIME: _____
LOCATION: _____

Did it smell?
☐ Yes ☐ No

IF YES, CHECK ALL THAT APPLY
- ☐ cheesy
- ☐ beany
- ☐ eggy
- ☐ oniony
- ☐ malty
- ☐ musty
- ☐ nutty
- ☐ skunky
- ☐ sulfur
- ☐ spicy
- ☐ pungent
- ☐ earthy
- ☐ prune
- ☐ cabbage
- ☐ funk
- ☐ taco

Smell-O-meter
(fill in the boxes)

not too bad ⟹ eye-watering

DID YOU TAKE OWNERSHIP? ☐ Yes ☐ No
☐ Blamed dog

fill in to appropriate level

- ninja
- quack
- blast
- engine
- nuclear

NOISE LEVEL

Any witnesses? ☐ Yes ☐ No

IF YES, who? _____
REACTION? _____

DRAW YOUR FART ←

OTHER NOTES: _____

FART

DATE: _____
TIME: _____
LOCATION: _____

Did it smell? ☐ Yes ☐ No

Smell-O-meter
(fill in the boxes)

not too bad ➡ eye-watering

IF YES, CHECK ALL THAT APPLY
- ☐ cheesy
- ☐ beany
- ☐ eggy
- ☐ oniony
- ☐ malty
- ☐ musty
- ☐ nutty
- ☐ skunky
- ☐ sulfur
- ☐ spicy
- ☐ pungent
- ☐ earthy
- ☐ prune
- ☐ cabbage
- ☐ funk
- ☐ taco

DID YOU TAKE OWNERSHIP? ☐ Yes ☐ No ☐ Blamed dog

NOISE LEVEL
(fill in to appropriate level)
- ninja
- quack
- blast
- engine
- nuclear

Any witnesses? ☐ Yes ☐ No
If YES, who? _____
REACTION? _____

DRAW YOUR FART ⬅

OTHER NOTES: _____

FART

DATE: _____
TIME: _____
LOCATION: _____

Did it smell?
☐ Yes ☐ No

IF YES, CHECK ALL THAT APPLY
- ☐ cheesy
- ☐ beany
- ☐ eggy
- ☐ oniony
- ☐ malty
- ☐ musty
- ☐ nutty
- ☐ skunky
- ☐ sulfur
- ☐ spicy
- ☐ pungent
- ☐ earthy
- ☐ prune
- ☐ cabbage
- ☐ funk
- ☐ taco

Smell-O-meter
(fill in the boxes)

not too bad ⇒ eye-watering

DID YOU TAKE OWNERSHIP? ☐ Yes ☐ No
☐ Blamed dog

fill in to appropriate level — ninja / quack / blast / engine / nuclear

NOISE LEVEL

Any witnesses? ☐ Yes ☐ No
If yes, who? _____
REACTION? _____

DRAW YOUR FART ←

OTHER NOTES: _____

FART

DATE: _____
TIME: _____
LOCATION: _____

Did it smell?
☐ Yes ☐ No

IF YES, CHECK ALL THAT APPLY
- ☐ cheesy
- ☐ beany
- ☐ eggy
- ☐ oniony
- ☐ malty
- ☐ musty
- ☐ nutty
- ☐ skunky
- ☐ sulfur
- ☐ spicy
- ☐ pungent
- ☐ earthy
- ☐ prune
- ☐ cabbage
- ☐ funk
- ☐ taco

Smell-O-meter
(fill in the boxes)

not too bad ⟹ eye-watering

DID YOU TAKE OWNERSHIP? ☐ Yes ☐ No ☐ Blamed dog

fill in to appropriate level

ninja | quack | blast | engine | nuclear

NOISE LEVEL

Any witnesses? ☐ Yes ☐ No
If YES, who? _____
REACTION? _____

DRAW YOUR FART ←

OTHER NOTES: _____

FART

DATE:
TIME:
LOCATION:

Did it smell?
☐ Yes ☐ No

Smell-O-meter
(fill in the boxes)

not too bad ⟶ eye-watering

DID YOU TAKE OWNERSHIP? ☐ Yes ☐ No ☐ Blamed dog

IF YES, CHECK ALL THAT APPLY
- ☐ cheesy
- ☐ beany
- ☐ eggy
- ☐ oniony
- ☐ malty
- ☐ musty
- ☐ nutty
- ☐ skunky
- ☐ sulfur
- ☐ spicy
- ☐ pungent
- ☐ earthy
- ☐ prune
- ☐ cabbage
- ☐ funk
- ☐ taco

fill in to appropriate level

quack · blast · engine · ninja · nuclear

NOISE LEVEL

Any witnesses? ☐ Yes ☐ No
If YES, who?
REACTION?

DRAW YOUR FART ←

OTHER NOTES:

FART

DATE: _____
TIME: _____
LOCATION: _____

Did it smell?
☐ Yes ☐ No

IF YES, CHECK ALL THAT APPLY
- ☐ cheesy
- ☐ beany
- ☐ eggy
- ☐ oniony
- ☐ malty
- ☐ musty
- ☐ nutty
- ☐ skunky
- ☐ sulfur
- ☐ spicy
- ☐ pungent
- ☐ earthy
- ☐ prune
- ☐ cabbage
- ☐ funk
- ☐ taco

Smell-O-meter
(fill in the boxes)

not too bad ⇒ eye-watering

DID YOU TAKE OWNERSHIP? ☐ Yes ☐ No
☐ Blamed dog

NOISE LEVEL
fill in to appropriate level
- ninja
- quack
- blast
- engine
- nuclear

Any witnesses? ☐ Yes ☐ No
If YES, who? _____
REACTION? _____

DRAW YOUR FART ←

OTHER NOTES: _____

FART

DATE:
TIME:
LOCATION:

Did it smell?
☐ Yes ☐ No

Smell-O-meter
(fill in the boxes)

not too bad → eye-watering

IF YES, CHECK ALL THAT APPLY
- ☐ cheesy
- ☐ beany
- ☐ eggy
- ☐ oniony
- ☐ malty
- ☐ musty
- ☐ nutty
- ☐ skunky
- ☐ sulfur
- ☐ spicy
- ☐ pungent
- ☐ earthy
- ☐ prune
- ☐ cabbage
- ☐ funk
- ☐ taco

DID YOU TAKE OWNERSHIP? ☐ Yes ☐ No ☐ Blamed dog

fill in to appropriate level

- ninja
- quack
- blast
- engine
- nuclear

NOISE LEVEL

Any witnesses? ☐ Yes ☐ No
If YES, who? ....
REACTION? ....

DRAW YOUR FART ←

OTHER NOTES: ....

FART

DATE: _____

TIME: _____

LOCATION: _____

Did it smell?
☐ Yes ☐ No

Smell-O-meter
(fill in the boxes)

not too bad ⟶ eye-watering

IF YES, CHECK ALL THAT APPLY
- ☐ cheesy
- ☐ beany
- ☐ eggy
- ☐ oniony
- ☐ malty
- ☐ musty
- ☐ nutty
- ☐ skunky
- ☐ sulfur
- ☐ spicy
- ☐ pungent
- ☐ earthy
- ☐ prune
- ☐ cabbage
- ☐ funk
- ☐ taco

DID YOU TAKE OWNERSHIP? ☐ Yes ☐ No ☐ Blamed dog

fill in to appropriate level: ninja / quack / blast / engine / nuclear

NOISE LEVEL

Any witnesses? ☐ Yes ☐ No

If YES, who? _____
REACTION? _____

DRAW YOUR FART ⬅

OTHER NOTES: _____

FART

DATE:

TIME:

LOCATION:

Did it smell? ☐ Yes ☐ No

IF YES, CHECK ALL THAT APPLY
- ☐ cheesy
- ☐ beany
- ☐ eggy
- ☐ oniony
- ☐ malty
- ☐ musty
- ☐ nutty
- ☐ skunky
- ☐ sulfur
- ☐ spicy
- ☐ pungent
- ☐ earthy
- ☐ prune
- ☐ cabbage
- ☐ funk
- ☐ taco

Smell-O-meter
(fill in the boxes)

not too bad ⟹ eye-watering

DID YOU TAKE OWNERSHIP? ☐ Yes ☐ No ☐ Blamed dog

NOISE LEVEL
fill in to appropriate level
- ninja
- quack
- blast
- engine
- nuclear

Any witnesses? ☐ Yes ☐ No

If YES, who?

REACTION?

DRAW YOUR FART ←

OTHER NOTES:

FART #　◯

DATE: _____
TIME: _____
LOCATION: _____

Did it smell?
☐ Yes ☐ No

Smell-O-meter
(fill in the boxes)

[ ][ ][ ][ ][ ][ ][ ][ ][ ][ ][ ][ ][ ][ ]

not too bad ⟹ eye-watering

IF YES, CHECK ALL THAT APPLY
- ☐ cheesy
- ☐ beany
- ☐ eggy
- ☐ oniony
- ☐ malty
- ☐ musty
- ☐ nutty
- ☐ skunky
- ☐ sulfur
- ☐ spicy
- ☐ pungent
- ☐ earthy
- ☐ prune
- ☐ cabbage
- ☐ funk
- ☐ taco

DID YOU TAKE OWNERSHIP? ☐ Yes ☐ No
☐ Blamed dog

NOISE LEVEL
fill in to appropriate level

- ninja
- quack
- blast
- engine
- nuclear

Any witnesses?
☐ Yes ☐ No

IF YES, who? _____
REACTION? _____

DRAW YOUR FART ←

OTHER NOTES: _____

FART

DATE:

TIME:

LOCATION:

Did it smell?
☐ Yes ☐ No

Smell-O-meter
(fill in the boxes)

not too bad ➡ eye-watering

IF YES, CHECK ALL THAT APPLY
- ☐ cheesy
- ☐ beany
- ☐ eggy
- ☐ oniony
- ☐ malty
- ☐ musty
- ☐ nutty
- ☐ skunky
- ☐ sulfur
- ☐ spicy
- ☐ pungent
- ☐ earthy
- ☐ prune
- ☐ cabbage
- ☐ funk
- ☐ taco

DID YOU TAKE OWNERSHIP? ☐ Yes ☐ No ☐ Blamed dog

fill in to appropriate level

- quack
- blast
- engine
- ninja
- nuclear

NOISE LEVEL

Any witnesses? ☐ Yes ☐ No

If YES, who?

REACTION?

DRAW YOUR FART ⬅

OTHER NOTES:

FART

DATE: _____
TIME: _____
LOCATION: _____

Did it smell?
☐ Yes ☐ No

Smell-O-meter
(fill in the boxes)

not too bad ➡ eye-watering

IF YES, CHECK ALL THAT APPLY
- ☐ cheesy
- ☐ beany
- ☐ eggy
- ☐ oniony
- ☐ malty
- ☐ musty
- ☐ nutty
- ☐ skunky
- ☐ sulfur
- ☐ spicy
- ☐ pungent
- ☐ earthy
- ☐ prune
- ☐ cabbage
- ☐ funk
- ☐ taco

DID YOU TAKE OWNERSHIP? ☐ Yes ☐ No ☐ Blamed dog

fill in to appropriate level

quack | blast | engine
ninja | | nuclear

NOISE LEVEL

Any witnesses? ■ Yes ■ No
If YES, who? _____
REACTION? _____

DRAW YOUR FART ←

OTHER NOTES: _____

FART

DATE:
TIME:
LOCATION:

Did it smell?
☐ Yes ☐ No

Smell-O-meter
(fill in the boxes)

not too bad → eye-watering

IF YES, CHECK ALL THAT APPLY
- ☐ cheesy
- ☐ beany
- ☐ eggy
- ☐ oniony
- ☐ malty
- ☐ musty
- ☐ nutty
- ☐ skunky
- ☐ sulfur
- ☐ spicy
- ☐ pungent
- ☐ earthy
- ☐ prune
- ☐ cabbage
- ☐ funk
- ☐ taco

DID YOU TAKE OWNERSHIP? ☐ Yes ☐ No ☐ Blamed dog

fill in to appropriate level

- ninja
- quack
- blast
- engine
- nuclear

NOISE LEVEL

Any witnesses? ☐ Yes ☐ No

IF YES, who? ....
REACTION? ....

DRAW YOUR FART ←

OTHER NOTES: ....

FART

DATE:

TIME:

LOCATION:

Did it smell?
☐ Yes ☐ No

Smell-O-meter
(fill in the boxes)

not too bad ⟹ eye-watering

IF YES, CHECK ALL THAT APPLY

☐ cheesy
☐ beany
☐ eggy
☐ oniony
☐ malty
☐ musty
☐ nutty
☐ skunky
☐ sulfur
☐ spicy
☐ pungent
☐ earthy
☐ prune
☐ cabbage
☐ funk
☐ taco

DID YOU TAKE OWNERSHIP? ☐ Yes ☐ No
☐ Blamed dog

NOISE LEVEL
fill in to appropriate level

- ninja
- quack
- blast
- engine
- nuclear

Any witnesses? ■ Yes ■ No

If YES, who?
REACTION?

DRAW YOUR FART ⬅

OTHER NOTES:

FART

DATE: _____
TIME: _____
LOCATION: _____

Smell-O-meter
(fill in the boxes)

not too bad ➡ eye-watering

Did it smell? ☐ Yes ☐ No

IF YES, CHECK ALL THAT APPLY
- ☐ cheesy
- ☐ beany
- ☐ eggy
- ☐ oniony
- ☐ malty
- ☐ musty
- ☐ nutty
- ☐ skunky
- ☐ sulfur
- ☐ spicy
- ☐ pungent
- ☐ earthy
- ☐ prune
- ☐ cabbage
- ☐ funk
- ☐ taco

DID YOU TAKE OWNERSHIP? ☐ Yes ☐ No ☐ Blamed dog

NOISE LEVEL
fill in to appropriate level

- ninja
- quack
- blast
- engine
- nuclear

Any witnesses? ☐ Yes ☐ No
If YES, who? _____
REACTION? _____

DRAW YOUR FART ⬅

OTHER NOTES: _____

FART

DATE: _____
TIME: _____
LOCATION: _____

Did it smell?
☐ Yes ☐ No

IF YES, CHECK ALL THAT APPLY
- ☐ cheesy
- ☐ beany
- ☐ eggy
- ☐ oniony
- ☐ malty
- ☐ musty
- ☐ nutty
- ☐ skunky
- ☐ sulfur
- ☐ spicy
- ☐ pungent
- ☐ earthy
- ☐ prune
- ☐ cabbage
- ☐ funk
- ☐ taco

Smell-O-meter
(fill in the boxes)

not too bad ⟹ eye-watering

DID YOU TAKE OWNERSHIP? ☐ Yes ☐ No ☐ Blamed dog

fill in to appropriate level

ninja | quack | blast | engine | nuclear

NOISE LEVEL

Any witnesses? ☐ Yes ☐ No

If YES, who? _____
REACTION? _____

DRAW YOUR FART ←

OTHER NOTES: _____

FART

DATE: _____
TIME: _____
LOCATION: _____

Did it smell?
☐ Yes ☐ No

Smell-O-meter
(fill in the boxes)

not too bad ➡ eye-watering

DID YOU TAKE OWNERSHIP? ☐ Yes ☐ No ☐ Blamed dog

IF YES, CHECK ALL THAT APPLY
- ☐ cheesy
- ☐ beany
- ☐ eggy
- ☐ oniony
- ☐ malty
- ☐ musty
- ☐ nutty
- ☐ skunky
- ☐ sulfur
- ☐ spicy
- ☐ pungent
- ☐ earthy
- ☐ prune
- ☐ cabbage
- ☐ funk
- ☐ taco

NOISE LEVEL
fill in to appropriate level: quack, blast, engine, ninja, nuclear

Any witnesses?
☐ Yes ☐ No

IF YES, who? _____
REACTION? _____

DRAW YOUR FART ←

OTHER NOTES: _____

FART # ◯

DATE: _____
TIME: _____
LOCATION: _____

Did it smell?
☐ Yes ☐ No

IF YES, CHECK ALL THAT APPLY
- ☐ cheesy
- ☐ beany
- ☐ eggy
- ☐ oniony
- ☐ malty
- ☐ musty
- ☐ nutty
- ☐ skunky
- ☐ sulfur
- ☐ spicy
- ☐ pungent
- ☐ earthy
- ☐ prune
- ☐ cabbage
- ☐ funk
- ☐ taco

Smell-O-meter
(fill in the boxes)

[ ][ ][ ][ ][ ][ ][ ][ ][ ][ ][ ][ ]

not too bad ⟹ eye-watering

DID YOU TAKE OWNERSHIP? ☐ Yes ☐ No ☐ Blamed dog

fill in to appropriate level

ninja | quack | blast | engine | nuclear

NOISE LEVEL

Any witnesses? ☐ Yes ☐ No
If YES, who? _____
REACTION? _____

DRAW YOUR FART ←

OTHER NOTES: _____

FART

DATE: _____
TIME: _____
LOCATION: _____

Did it smell?
☐ Yes ☐ No

IF YES, CHECK ALL THAT APPLY
- ☐ cheesy
- ☐ beany
- ☐ eggy
- ☐ oniony
- ☐ malty
- ☐ musty
- ☐ nutty
- ☐ skunky
- ☐ sulfur
- ☐ spicy
- ☐ pungent
- ☐ earthy
- ☐ prune
- ☐ cabbage
- ☐ funk
- ☐ taco

Smell-O-meter
(fill in the boxes)

not too bad ➡ eye-watering

DID YOU TAKE OWNERSHIP? ☐ Yes ☐ No
☐ Blamed dog

NOISE LEVEL
fill in to appropriate level
- ninja
- quack
- blast
- engine
- nuclear

Any witnesses? ☐ Yes ☐ No
IF YES, who? _____
REACTION? _____

DRAW YOUR FART ⬅

OTHER NOTES: _____

FART

DATE: _____
TIME: _____
LOCATION: _____

Did it smell?
☐ Yes ☐ No

Smell-O-meter
(fill in the boxes)

not too bad ⟹ eye-watering

IF YES, CHECK ALL THAT APPLY
- ☐ cheesy
- ☐ beany
- ☐ eggy
- ☐ oniony
- ☐ malty
- ☐ musty
- ☐ nutty
- ☐ skunky
- ☐ sulfur
- ☐ spicy
- ☐ pungent
- ☐ earthy
- ☐ prune
- ☐ cabbage
- ☐ funk
- ☐ taco

DID YOU TAKE OWNERSHIP? ☐ Yes ☐ No ☐ Blamed dog

NOISE LEVEL
(fill in to appropriate level)

ninja · quack · blast · engine · nuclear

Any witnesses? ☐ Yes ☐ No
IF YES, who? _____
REACTION? _____

DRAW YOUR FART ←

OTHER NOTES: _____

FART

DATE: _____
TIME: _____
LOCATION: _____

Did it smell?
☐ Yes ☐ No

IF YES, CHECK ALL THAT APPLY
- ☐ cheesy
- ☐ beany
- ☐ eggy
- ☐ oniony
- ☐ malty
- ☐ musty
- ☐ nutty
- ☐ skunky
- ☐ sulfur
- ☐ spicy
- ☐ pungent
- ☐ earthy
- ☐ prune
- ☐ cabbage
- ☐ funk
- ☐ taco

Smell-O-meter
(fill in the boxes)

not too bad ➡ eye-watering

DID YOU TAKE OWNERSHIP? ☐ Yes ☐ No ☐ Blamed dog

NOISE LEVEL
fill in to appropriate level
- ninja
- quack
- blast
- engine
- nuclear

Any witnesses? ☐ Yes ☐ No
If YES, who? _____
REACTION? _____

DRAW YOUR FART ⬅

OTHER NOTES: _____

FART

DATE:

TIME:

LOCATION:

Did it smell?
☐ Yes ☐ No

Smell-O-meter
(fill in the boxes)

not too bad ⟶ eye-watering

IF YES, CHECK ALL THAT APPLY
- ☐ cheesy
- ☐ beany
- ☐ eggy
- ☐ oniony
- ☐ malty
- ☐ musty
- ☐ nutty
- ☐ skunky
- ☐ sulfur
- ☐ spicy
- ☐ pungent
- ☐ earthy
- ☐ prune
- ☐ cabbage
- ☐ funk
- ☐ taco

DID YOU TAKE OWNERSHIP? ☐ Yes ☐ No ☐ Blamed dog

fill in to appropriate level — ninja, quack, blast, engine, nuclear

NOISE LEVEL

Any witnesses? ☐ Yes ☐ No
If YES, who?
REACTION?

DRAW YOUR FART ←

OTHER NOTES:

FART

DATE: _____
TIME: _____
LOCATION: _____

Did it smell?
☐ Yes ☐ No

Smell-O-meter
(fill in the boxes)

not too bad ➡ eye-watering

IF YES, CHECK ALL THAT APPLY
- ☐ cheesy
- ☐ beany
- ☐ eggy
- ☐ oniony
- ☐ malty
- ☐ musty
- ☐ nutty
- ☐ skunky
- ☐ sulfur
- ☐ spicy
- ☐ pungent
- ☐ earthy
- ☐ prune
- ☐ cabbage
- ☐ funk
- ☐ taco

DID YOU TAKE OWNERSHIP? ☐ Yes ☐ No ☐ Blamed dog

fill in to appropriate level — ninja / quack / blast / engine / nuclear

NOISE LEVEL

Any witnesses? ☐ Yes ☐ No
If YES, who? _____
REACTION? _____

DRAW YOUR FART ←

OTHER NOTES: _____

FART

DATE: _____
TIME: _____
LOCATION: _____

Did it smell?
☐ Yes ☐ No

IF YES, CHECK ALL THAT APPLY
- ☐ cheesy
- ☐ beany
- ☐ eggy
- ☐ oniony
- ☐ malty
- ☐ musty
- ☐ nutty
- ☐ skunky
- ☐ sulfur
- ☐ spicy
- ☐ pungent
- ☐ earthy
- ☐ prune
- ☐ cabbage
- ☐ funk
- ☐ taco

Smell-O-meter
(fill in the boxes)

not too bad ➡ eye-watering

DID YOU TAKE OWNERSHIP? ☐ Yes ☐ No ☐ Blamed dog

NOISE LEVEL
fill in to appropriate level
- ninja
- quack
- blast
- engine
- nuclear

Any witnesses? ■ Yes ■ No
If YES, who? _____
REACTION? _____

DRAW YOUR FART ←

OTHER NOTES: _____

FART

DATE: _____ **TIME:** _____ **LOCATION:** _____

Did it smell?
☐ Yes ☐ No

IF YES, CHECK ALL THAT APPLY
- ☐ cheesy
- ☐ beany
- ☐ eggy
- ☐ oniony
- ☐ malty
- ☐ musty
- ☐ nutty
- ☐ skunky
- ☐ sulfur
- ☐ spicy
- ☐ pungent
- ☐ earthy
- ☐ prune
- ☐ cabbage
- ☐ funk
- ☐ taco

Smell-O-meter
(fill in the boxes)

not too bad ⟹ eye-watering

DID YOU TAKE OWNERSHIP? ☐ Yes ☐ No ☐ Blamed dog

fill in to appropriate level

NOISE LEVEL
- ninja
- quack
- blast
- engine
- nuclear

Any witnesses? ☐ Yes ☐ No

If YES, who? _____
REACTION? _____

DRAW YOUR FART ←

OTHER NOTES: _____

FART

DATE: _____
TIME: _____
LOCATION: _____

Did it smell?
☐ Yes ☐ No

Smell-O-meter
(fill in the boxes)

☐☐☐☐☐☐☐☐☐☐

not too bad ⟹ eye-watering

DID YOU TAKE OWNERSHIP? ☐ Yes ☐ No
☐ Blamed dog

IF YES, CHECK ALL THAT APPLY
- ☐ cheesy
- ☐ beany
- ☐ eggy
- ☐ oniony
- ☐ malty
- ☐ musty
- ☐ nutty
- ☐ skunky
- ☐ sulfur
- ☐ spicy
- ☐ pungent
- ☐ earthy
- ☐ prune
- ☐ cabbage
- ☐ funk
- ☐ taco

NOISE LEVEL
fill in to appropriate level

- ninja
- quack
- blast
- engine
- nuclear

Any witnesses?
☐ Yes ☐ No

If YES, who? _____
REACTION? _____

DRAW YOUR FART ←

OTHER NOTES: _____

FART # ◯

DATE: _____
TIME: _____
LOCATION: _____

Did it smell?
☐ Yes ☐ No

Smell-O-meter
(fill in the boxes)

[ ][ ][ ][ ][ ][ ][ ][ ][ ][ ][ ][ ]

not too bad ⟹ eye-watering

IF YES, CHECK ALL THAT APPLY
- ☐ cheesy
- ☐ beany
- ☐ eggy
- ☐ oniony
- ☐ malty
- ☐ musty
- ☐ nutty
- ☐ skunky
- ☐ sulfur
- ☐ spicy
- ☐ pungent
- ☐ earthy
- ☐ prune
- ☐ cabbage
- ☐ funk
- ☐ taco

DID YOU TAKE OWNERSHIP?
☐ Yes ☐ No
☐ Blamed dog

NOISE LEVEL
fill in to appropriate level
- ninja
- quack
- blast
- engine
- nuclear

Any witnesses?
☐ Yes ☐ No

IF YES, who? _____
REACTION? _____

DRAW YOUR FART ←

OTHER NOTES: _____

FART # ◯

DATE: _____
TIME: _____
LOCATION: _____

Did it smell?
☐ Yes ☐ No

IF YES, CHECK ALL THAT APPLY
- ☐ cheesy
- ☐ beany
- ☐ eggy
- ☐ oniony
- ☐ malty
- ☐ musty
- ☐ nutty
- ☐ skunky
- ☐ sulfur
- ☐ spicy
- ☐ pungent
- ☐ earthy
- ☐ prune
- ☐ cabbage
- ☐ funk
- ☐ taco

Smell-O-meter
(fill in the boxes)

not too bad ⟹ eye-watering

DID YOU TAKE OWNERSHIP? ☐ Yes ☐ No
☐ Blamed dog

fill in to appropriate level

- ninja
- quack
- blast
- engine
- nuclear

NOISE LEVEL

Any witnesses?
■ Yes ■ No

IF YES, who? _____
REACTION? _____

DRAW YOUR FART ←

OTHER NOTES: _____

FART # ____

DATE: ____
TIME: ____
LOCATION: ____

Did it smell?
☐ Yes ☐ No

IF YES, CHECK ALL THAT APPLY
- ☐ cheesy
- ☐ beany
- ☐ eggy
- ☐ oniony
- ☐ malty
- ☐ musty
- ☐ nutty
- ☐ skunky
- ☐ sulfur
- ☐ spicy
- ☐ pungent
- ☐ earthy
- ☐ prune
- ☐ cabbage
- ☐ funk
- ☐ taco

Smell-O-meter
(fill in the boxes)

not too bad ⟹ eye-watering

DID YOU TAKE OWNERSHIP? ☐ Yes ☐ No ☐ Blamed dog

fill in to appropriate level

- quack
- blast
- engine
- ninja
- nuclear

NOISE LEVEL

Any witnesses? ☐ Yes ☐ No

If YES, who? ____
REACTION? ____

DRAW YOUR FART ←

OTHER NOTES: ____

FART

DATE: _____
TIME: _____
LOCATION: _____

Did it smell?
☐ Yes ☐ No

IF YES, CHECK ALL THAT APPLY
- ☐ cheesy
- ☐ beany
- ☐ eggy
- ☐ oniony
- ☐ malty
- ☐ musty
- ☐ nutty
- ☐ skunky
- ☐ sulfur
- ☐ spicy
- ☐ pungent
- ☐ earthy
- ☐ prune
- ☐ cabbage
- ☐ funk
- ☐ taco

Smell-O-meter
(fill in the boxes)

not too bad ⟹ eye-watering

DID YOU TAKE OWNERSHIP? ☐ Yes ☐ No
☐ Blamed dog

fill in to appropriate level

- ninja
- quack
- blast
- engine
- nuclear

NOISE LEVEL

Any witnesses? ☐ Yes ☐ No
If YES, who? _____
REACTION? _____

DRAW YOUR FART ←

OTHER NOTES: _____

FART

DATE: _____
TIME: _____
LOCATION: _____

Did it smell?
☐ Yes ☐ No

Smell-O-meter
(fill in the boxes)

☐☐☐☐☐☐☐☐☐☐☐☐☐

not too bad ➡ eye-watering

IF YES, CHECK ALL THAT APPLY
- ☐ cheesy
- ☐ beany
- ☐ eggy
- ☐ oniony
- ☐ malty
- ☐ musty
- ☐ nutty
- ☐ skunky
- ☐ sulfur
- ☐ spicy
- ☐ pungent
- ☐ earthy
- ☐ prune
- ☐ cabbage
- ☐ funk
- ☐ taco

DID YOU TAKE OWNERSHIP? ☐ Yes ☐ No
☐ Blamed dog

NOISE LEVEL
fill in to appropriate level
- ninja
- quack
- blast
- engine
- nuclear

Any witnesses? ☐ Yes ☐ No
If YES, who? _____
REACTION? _____

DRAW YOUR FART ⬅

OTHER NOTES: _____

FART

DATE: _____
TIME: _____
LOCATION: _____

Did it smell?
☐ Yes ☐ No

IF YES, CHECK ALL THAT APPLY
- ☐ cheesy
- ☐ beany
- ☐ eggy
- ☐ oniony
- ☐ malty
- ☐ musty
- ☐ nutty
- ☐ skunky
- ☐ sulfur
- ☐ spicy
- ☐ pungent
- ☐ earthy
- ☐ prune
- ☐ cabbage
- ☐ funk
- ☐ taco

Smell-O-meter
(fill in the boxes)

not too bad ⟹ eye-watering

DID YOU TAKE OWNERSHIP? ☐ Yes ☐ No ☐ Blamed dog

fill in to appropriate level

ninja | quack | blast | engine | nuclear

NOISE LEVEL

Any witnesses? ☐ Yes ☐ No

IF YES, who? _____
REACTION? _____

DRAW YOUR FART ←

OTHER NOTES: _____

FART

DATE: _____
TIME: _____
LOCATION: _____

Did it smell?
☐ Yes ☐ No

IF YES, CHECK ALL THAT APPLY
- ☐ cheesy
- ☐ beany
- ☐ eggy
- ☐ oniony
- ☐ malty
- ☐ musty
- ☐ nutty
- ☐ skunky
- ☐ sulfur
- ☐ spicy
- ☐ pungent
- ☐ earthy
- ☐ prune
- ☐ cabbage
- ☐ funk
- ☐ taco

Smell-O-meter
(fill in the boxes)

not too bad ⟶ eye-watering

DID YOU TAKE OWNERSHIP? ☐ Yes ☐ No ☐ Blamed dog

NOISE LEVEL
fill in to appropriate level
- ninja
- quack
- blast
- engine
- nuclear

Any witnesses? ☐ Yes ☐ No
If YES, who? _____
REACTION? _____

DRAW YOUR FART ←

OTHER NOTES: _____

FART # ◯

DATE: _____

TIME: _____

LOCATION: _____

Did it smell?
☐ Yes ☐ No

Smell-O-meter
(fill in the boxes)

☐☐☐☐☐☐☐☐☐☐☐☐

not too bad ⟶ eye-watering

IF YES, CHECK ALL THAT APPLY
- ☐ cheesy
- ☐ beany
- ☐ eggy
- ☐ oniony
- ☐ malty
- ☐ musty
- ☐ nutty
- ☐ skunky
- ☐ sulfur
- ☐ spicy
- ☐ pungent
- ☐ earthy
- ☐ prune
- ☐ cabbage
- ☐ funk
- ☐ taco

DID YOU TAKE OWNERSHIP? ☐ Yes ☐ No ☐ Blamed dog

fill in to appropriate level

ninja • quack • blast • engine • nuclear

NOISE LEVEL

Any witnesses?
■ Yes ■ No

If YES, who? _____

REACTION? _____

DRAW YOUR FART ←

OTHER NOTES: _____

FART # ◯

DATE: _____
TIME: _____
LOCATION: _____

Did it smell?
☐ Yes ☐ No

Smell-O-meter
(fill in the boxes)

not too bad ⟹ eye-watering

IF YES, CHECK ALL THAT APPLY
- ☐ cheesy
- ☐ beany
- ☐ eggy
- ☐ oniony
- ☐ malty
- ☐ musty
- ☐ nutty
- ☐ skunky
- ☐ sulfur
- ☐ spicy
- ☐ pungent
- ☐ earthy
- ☐ prune
- ☐ cabbage
- ☐ funk
- ☐ taco

DID YOU TAKE OWNERSHIP? ☐ Yes ☐ No ☐ Blamed dog

fill in to appropriate level

- ninja
- quack
- blast
- engine
- nuclear

NOISE LEVEL

Any witnesses? ☐ Yes ☐ No
If YES, who? _____
REACTION? _____

DRAW YOUR FART ←

OTHER NOTES: _____

FART

DATE: _____
TIME: _____
LOCATION: _____

Did it smell?
☐ Yes ☐ No

IF YES, CHECK ALL THAT APPLY
- ☐ cheesy
- ☐ beany
- ☐ eggy
- ☐ oniony
- ☐ malty
- ☐ musty
- ☐ nutty
- ☐ skunky
- ☐ sulfur
- ☐ spicy
- ☐ pungent
- ☐ earthy
- ☐ prune
- ☐ cabbage
- ☐ funk
- ☐ taco

Smell-O-meter
(fill in the boxes)

not too bad ⟹ eye-watering

DID YOU TAKE OWNERSHIP? ☐ Yes ☐ No
☐ Blamed dog

NOISE LEVEL
fill in to appropriate level
- ninja
- quack
- blast
- engine
- nuclear

Any witnesses? ☐ Yes ☐ No
IF YES, who? _____
REACTION? _____

DRAW YOUR FART ←

OTHER NOTES: _____

FART

DATE: _____
TIME: _____
LOCATION: _____

Did it smell?
☐ Yes ☐ No

Smell-O-meter
(fill in the boxes)

☐☐☐☐☐☐☐☐☐☐☐☐☐☐

not too bad ➡ eye-watering

DID YOU TAKE OWNERSHIP? ☐ Yes ☐ No
☐ Blamed dog

IF YES, CHECK ALL THAT APPLY
☐ cheesy
☐ beany
☐ eggy
☐ oniony
☐ malty
☐ musty
☐ nutty
☐ skunky
☐ sulfur
☐ spicy
☐ pungent
☐ earthy
☐ prune
☐ cabbage
☐ funk
☐ taco

NOISE LEVEL
fill in to appropriate level

- ninja
- quack
- blast
- engine
- nuclear

Any witnesses?
☐ Yes ☐ No

If YES, who? _____
REACTION? _____

DRAW YOUR FART ⬅

OTHER NOTES: _____

FART

DATE: _____
TIME: _____
LOCATION: _____

Did it smell?
☐ Yes ☐ No

IF YES, CHECK ALL THAT APPLY
- ☐ cheesy
- ☐ beany
- ☐ eggy
- ☐ oniony
- ☐ malty
- ☐ musty
- ☐ nutty
- ☐ skunky
- ☐ sulfur
- ☐ spicy
- ☐ pungent
- ☐ earthy
- ☐ prune
- ☐ cabbage
- ☐ funk
- ☐ taco

Smell-O-meter
(fill in the boxes)

not too bad ⟹ eye-watering

DID YOU TAKE OWNERSHIP? ☐ Yes ☐ No ☐ Blamed dog

fill in to appropriate level

- ninja
- quack
- blast
- engine
- nuclear

NOISE LEVEL

Any witnesses? ☐ Yes ☐ No

If YES, who? _____
REACTION? _____

DRAW YOUR FART ←

OTHER NOTES: _____

FART

DATE: _____
TIME: _____
LOCATION: _____

Did it smell?
☐ Yes ☐ No

Smell-O-meter
(fill in the boxes)

not too bad ⟹ eye-watering

IF YES, CHECK ALL THAT APPLY
- ☐ cheesy
- ☐ beany
- ☐ eggy
- ☐ oniony
- ☐ malty
- ☐ musty
- ☐ nutty
- ☐ skunky
- ☐ sulfur
- ☐ spicy
- ☐ pungent
- ☐ earthy
- ☐ prune
- ☐ cabbage
- ☐ funk
- ☐ taco

DID YOU TAKE OWNERSHIP? ☐ Yes ☐ No
☐ Blamed dog

NOISE LEVEL
fill in to appropriate level
- ninja
- quack
- blast
- engine
- nuclear

Any witnesses? ☐ Yes ☐ No
If YES, who? _____
REACTION? _____

DRAW YOUR FART ←

OTHER NOTES: _____

FART

LOCATION:

DATE:

TIME:

Did it smell?
☐ Yes ☐ No

Smell-O-meter
(fill in the boxes)

not too bad ➡ eye-watering

IF YES, CHECK ALL THAT APPLY

- ☐ cheesy
- ☐ beany
- ☐ eggy
- ☐ oniony
- ☐ malty
- ☐ musty
- ☐ nutty
- ☐ skunky
- ☐ sulfur
- ☐ spicy
- ☐ pungent
- ☐ earthy
- ☐ prune
- ☐ cabbage
- ☐ funk
- ☐ taco

DID YOU TAKE OWNERSHIP? ☐ Yes ☐ No
☐ Blamed dog

fill in to appropriate level

quack · blast · engine
ninja · nuclear

NOISE LEVEL

Any witnesses?
☐ Yes ☐ No

If YES, who?
REACTION?

DRAW YOUR FART ⬅

OTHER NOTES:

FART

DATE: _____
TIME: _____
LOCATION: _____

Did it smell?
☐ Yes ☐ No

IF YES, CHECK ALL THAT APPLY
- ☐ cheesy
- ☐ beany
- ☐ eggy
- ☐ oniony
- ☐ malty
- ☐ musty
- ☐ nutty
- ☐ skunky
- ☐ sulfur
- ☐ spicy
- ☐ pungent
- ☐ earthy
- ☐ prune
- ☐ cabbage
- ☐ funk
- ☐ taco

Smell-O-meter
(fill in the boxes)

not too bad ⟹ eye-watering

DID YOU TAKE OWNERSHIP? ☐ Yes ☐ No
☐ Blamed dog

fill in to appropriate level

- ninja
- quack
- blast
- engine
- nuclear

NOISE LEVEL

Any witnesses? ☐ Yes ☐ No

If YES, who? _____
REACTION? _____

DRAW YOUR FART ←

OTHER NOTES: _____

FART

DATE:
TIME:
LOCATION:

Did it smell?
☐ Yes ☐ No

IF YES, CHECK ALL THAT APPLY
- ☐ cheesy
- ☐ beany
- ☐ eggy
- ☐ oniony
- ☐ malty
- ☐ musty
- ☐ nutty
- ☐ skunky
- ☐ sulfur
- ☐ spicy
- ☐ pungent
- ☐ earthy
- ☐ prune
- ☐ cabbage
- ☐ funk
- ☐ taco

Smell-O-meter
(fill in the boxes)

not too bad ➡ eye-watering

DID YOU TAKE OWNERSHIP? ☐ Yes ☐ No ☐ Blamed dog

NOISE LEVEL
fill in to appropriate level
- ninja
- quack
- blast
- engine
- nuclear

Any witnesses? ☐ Yes ☐ No
If YES, who?
REACTION?

DRAW YOUR FART ⬅

OTHER NOTES:

FART

DATE: _____
TIME: _____
LOCATION: _____

Did it smell?
☐ Yes ☐ No

Smell-O-meter
(fill in the boxes)

not too bad ⟶ eye-watering

IF YES, CHECK ALL THAT APPLY

☐ cheesy
☐ beany
☐ eggy
☐ oniony
☐ malty
☐ musty
☐ nutty
☐ skunky
☐ sulfur
☐ spicy
☐ pungent
☐ earthy
☐ prune
☐ cabbage
☐ funk
☐ taco

DID YOU TAKE OWNERSHIP? ☐ Yes ☐ No
☐ Blamed dog

NOISE LEVEL
fill in to appropriate level
- quack
- blast
- engine
- ninja
- nuclear

Any witnesses? ■ Yes ■ No
If YES, who? _____
REACTION? _____

DRAW YOUR FART ⬅

OTHER NOTES: _____

FART

DATE: _____

TIME: _____

LOCATION: _____

Did it smell?
☐ Yes ☐ No

IF YES, CHECK ALL THAT APPLY
- ☐ cheesy
- ☐ beany
- ☐ eggy
- ☐ oniony
- ☐ malty
- ☐ musty
- ☐ nutty
- ☐ skunky
- ☐ sulfur
- ☐ spicy
- ☐ pungent
- ☐ earthy
- ☐ prune
- ☐ cabbage
- ☐ funk
- ☐ taco

Smell-O-meter
(fill in the boxes)

not too bad ➡ eye-watering

DID YOU TAKE OWNERSHIP? ☐ Yes ☐ No ☐ Blamed dog

NOISE LEVEL
fill in to appropriate level
- ninja
- quack
- blast
- engine
- nuclear

Any witnesses? ☐ Yes ☐ No

If YES, who? _____
REACTION? _____

DRAW YOUR FART ⬅

OTHER NOTES: _____

FART

DATE: _____
TIME: _____
LOCATION: _____

Did it smell?
☐ Yes ☐ No

IF YES, CHECK ALL THAT APPLY
- ☐ cheesy
- ☐ beany
- ☐ eggy
- ☐ oniony
- ☐ malty
- ☐ musty
- ☐ nutty
- ☐ skunky
- ☐ sulfur
- ☐ spicy
- ☐ pungent
- ☐ earthy
- ☐ prune
- ☐ cabbage
- ☐ funk
- ☐ taco

Smell-O-meter
(fill in the boxes)

not too bad ⟹ eye-watering

DID YOU TAKE OWNERSHIP? ☐ Yes ☐ No
☐ Blamed dog

fill in to appropriate level:
- ninja
- quack
- blast
- engine
- nuclear

NOISE LEVEL

Any witnesses? ☐ Yes ☐ No

If YES, who? _____
REACTION? _____

DRAW YOUR FART ←

OTHER NOTES: _____

FART

DATE: _____
TIME: _____
LOCATION: _____

Did it smell?
☐ Yes ☐ No

Smell-O-meter
(fill in the boxes)

☐☐☐☐☐☐☐☐☐☐

not too bad ➡ eye-watering

DID YOU TAKE OWNERSHIP? ☐ Yes ☐ No
☐ Blamed dog

IF YES, CHECK ALL THAT APPLY
- ☐ cheesy
- ☐ beany
- ☐ eggy
- ☐ oniony
- ☐ malty
- ☐ musty
- ☐ nutty
- ☐ skunky
- ☐ sulfur
- ☐ spicy
- ☐ pungent
- ☐ earthy
- ☐ prune
- ☐ cabbage
- ☐ funk
- ☐ taco

NOISE LEVEL
fill in to appropriate level
- quack
- blast
- engine
- ninja
- nuclear

Any witnesses?
☐ Yes ☐ No

If YES, who? _____
REACTION? _____

DRAW YOUR FART ⬅

OTHER NOTES: _____

FART

DATE: _____

TIME: _____

LOCATION: _____

Did it smell?
☐ Yes ☐ No

IF YES, CHECK ALL THAT APPLY
- ☐ cheesy
- ☐ beany
- ☐ eggy
- ☐ oniony
- ☐ malty
- ☐ musty
- ☐ nutty
- ☐ skunky
- ☐ sulfur
- ☐ spicy
- ☐ pungent
- ☐ earthy
- ☐ prune
- ☐ cabbage
- ☐ funk
- ☐ taco

Smell-O-meter
(fill in the boxes)

not too bad ➡ eye-watering

DID YOU TAKE OWNERSHIP? ☐ Yes ☐ No
☐ Blamed dog

fill in to appropriate level

ninja / quack / blast / engine / nuclear

NOISE LEVEL

Any witnesses? ■ Yes ■ No

If YES, who? _____
REACTION? _____

DRAW YOUR FART ←

OTHER NOTES: _____

FART

DATE: _____
TIME: _____
LOCATION: _____

Did it smell?
☐ Yes ☐ No

Smell-O-meter
(fill in the boxes)

not too bad ➔ eye-watering

IF YES, CHECK ALL THAT APPLY
- ☐ cheesy
- ☐ beany
- ☐ eggy
- ☐ oniony
- ☐ malty
- ☐ musty
- ☐ nutty
- ☐ skunky
- ☐ sulfur
- ☐ spicy
- ☐ pungent
- ☐ earthy
- ☐ prune
- ☐ cabbage
- ☐ funk
- ☐ taco

DID YOU TAKE OWNERSHIP? ☐ Yes ☐ No ☐ Blamed dog

fill in to appropriate level

quack | blast | engine
ninja | | nuclear

NOISE LEVEL

Any witnesses? ☐ Yes ☐ No
If YES, who? _____
REACTION? _____

DRAW YOUR FART ←

OTHER NOTES: _____

FART

DATE: _____
TIME: _____
LOCATION: _____

Did it smell?
☐ Yes ☐ No

Smell-O-meter
(fill in the boxes)

not too bad ⟹ eye-watering

IF YES, CHECK ALL THAT APPLY
- ☐ cheesy
- ☐ beany
- ☐ eggy
- ☐ oniony
- ☐ malty
- ☐ musty
- ☐ nutty
- ☐ skunky
- ☐ sulfur
- ☐ spicy
- ☐ pungent
- ☐ earthy
- ☐ prune
- ☐ cabbage
- ☐ funk
- ☐ taco

DID YOU TAKE OWNERSHIP? ☐ Yes ☐ No
☐ Blamed dog

fill in to appropriate level

ninja | quack | blast | engine | nuclear

NOISE LEVEL

Any witnesses? ☐ Yes ☐ No
If YES, who? _____
REACTION? _____

DRAW YOUR FART ⬅

OTHER NOTES: _____

FART

DATE: _____
TIME: _____
LOCATION: _____

Did it smell?
☐ Yes ☐ No

IF YES, CHECK ALL THAT APPLY
- ☐ cheesy
- ☐ beany
- ☐ eggy
- ☐ oniony
- ☐ malty
- ☐ musty
- ☐ nutty
- ☐ skunky
- ☐ sulfur
- ☐ spicy
- ☐ pungent
- ☐ earthy
- ☐ prune
- ☐ cabbage
- ☐ funk
- ☐ taco

Smell-O-meter
(fill in the boxes)

not too bad ⟹ eye-watering

DID YOU TAKE OWNERSHIP? ☐ Yes ☐ No ☐ Blamed dog

NOISE LEVEL
fill in to appropriate level

- ninja
- quack
- blast
- engine
- nuclear

Any witnesses? ☐ Yes ☐ No

If YES, who? _____
REACTION? _____

DRAW YOUR FART ←

OTHER NOTES: _____

FART

DATE: _____
TIME: _____
LOCATION: _____

Did it smell?
☐ Yes ☐ No

Smell-O-meter
(fill in the boxes)

☐☐☐☐☐☐☐☐☐☐☐☐☐☐☐☐

not too bad ⟹ eye-watering

IF YES, CHECK ALL THAT APPLY
- ☐ cheesy
- ☐ beany
- ☐ eggy
- ☐ oniony
- ☐ malty
- ☐ musty
- ☐ nutty
- ☐ skunky
- ☐ sulfur
- ☐ spicy
- ☐ pungent
- ☐ earthy
- ☐ prune
- ☐ cabbage
- ☐ funk
- ☐ taco

DID YOU TAKE OWNERSHIP? ☐ Yes ☐ No
☐ Blamed dog

fill in to appropriate level

- quack
- blast
- engine
- ninja
- nuclear

NOISE LEVEL

Any witnesses? ☐ Yes ☐ No
If YES, who? _____
REACTION? _____

DRAW YOUR FART ⬅

OTHER NOTES: _____

FART

DATE: _____
TIME: _____
LOCATION: _____

Did it smell?
☐ Yes ☐ No

Smell-O-meter
(fill in the boxes)

not too bad ➡ eye-watering

IF YES, CHECK ALL THAT APPLY
- ☐ cheesy
- ☐ beany
- ☐ eggy
- ☐ oniony
- ☐ malty
- ☐ musty
- ☐ nutty
- ☐ skunky
- ☐ sulfur
- ☐ spicy
- ☐ pungent
- ☐ earthy
- ☐ prune
- ☐ cabbage
- ☐ funk
- ☐ taco

DID YOU TAKE OWNERSHIP? ☐ Yes ☐ No
☐ Blamed dog

fill in to appropriate level

- quack
- blast
- engine
- ninja
- nuclear

NOISE LEVEL

Any witnesses? ■ Yes ■ No
If YES, who? _____
REACTION? _____

DRAW YOUR FART ⬅

OTHER NOTES: _____

FART

DATE:
TIME:
LOCATION:

Did it smell?
☐ Yes ☐ No

Smell-O-meter
(fill in the boxes)

not too bad ➡ eye-watering

IF YES, CHECK ALL THAT APPLY
- ☐ cheesy
- ☐ beany
- ☐ eggy
- ☐ oniony
- ☐ malty
- ☐ musty
- ☐ nutty
- ☐ skunky
- ☐ sulfur
- ☐ spicy
- ☐ pungent
- ☐ earthy
- ☐ prune
- ☐ cabbage
- ☐ funk
- ☐ taco

DID YOU TAKE OWNERSHIP? ☐ Yes ☐ No ☐ Blamed dog

NOISE LEVEL
fill in to appropriate level
- ninja
- quack
- blast
- engine
- nuclear

Any witnesses? ☐ Yes ☐ No
If YES, who?
REACTION?

DRAW YOUR FART ⬅

OTHER NOTES:

FART

LOCATION:
TIME:
DATE:

Did it smell?
☐ Yes ☐ No

IF YES, CHECK ALL THAT APPLY
- ☐ cheesy
- ☐ beany
- ☐ eggy
- ☐ oniony
- ☐ malty
- ☐ musty
- ☐ nutty
- ☐ skunky
- ☐ sulfur
- ☐ spicy
- ☐ pungent
- ☐ earthy
- ☐ prune
- ☐ cabbage
- ☐ funk
- ☐ taco

Smell-O-meter
(fill in the boxes)

not too bad ⟹ eye-watering

DID YOU TAKE OWNERSHIP? ☐ Yes ☐ No ☐ Blamed dog

NOISE LEVEL
fill in to appropriate level
- ninja
- quack
- blast
- engine
- nuclear

Any witnesses? ☐ Yes ☐ No
If YES, who?
REACTION?

DRAW YOUR FART ←

OTHER NOTES:

FART

DATE: _____
TIME: _____
LOCATION: _____

Did it smell?
☐ Yes ☐ No

IF YES, CHECK ALL THAT APPLY
- ☐ cheesy
- ☐ beany
- ☐ eggy
- ☐ oniony
- ☐ malty
- ☐ musty
- ☐ nutty
- ☐ skunky
- ☐ sulfur
- ☐ spicy
- ☐ pungent
- ☐ earthy
- ☐ prune
- ☐ cabbage
- ☐ funk
- ☐ taco

Smell-O-meter
(fill in the boxes)

not too bad ⟹ eye-watering

DID YOU TAKE OWNERSHIP? ☐ Yes ☐ No ☐ Blamed dog

NOISE LEVEL
fill in to appropriate level
- ninja
- quack
- blast
- engine
- nuclear

Any witnesses? ☐ Yes ☐ No
IF YES, who? _____
REACTION? _____

DRAW YOUR FART ←

OTHER NOTES: _____

FART

DATE: _____
TIME: _____
LOCATION: _____

Did it smell?
☐ Yes ☐ No

Smell-O-meter
(fill in the boxes)

not too bad ➡ eye-watering

DID YOU TAKE OWNERSHIP? ☐ Yes ☐ No ☐ Blamed dog

IF YES, CHECK ALL THAT APPLY
- ☐ cheesy
- ☐ beany
- ☐ eggy
- ☐ oniony
- ☐ malty
- ☐ musty
- ☐ nutty
- ☐ skunky
- ☐ sulfur
- ☐ spicy
- ☐ pungent
- ☐ earthy
- ☐ prune
- ☐ cabbage
- ☐ funk
- ☐ taco

NOISE LEVEL
fill in to appropriate level
- quack
- blast
- engine
- ninja
- nuclear

Any witnesses? ☐ Yes ☐ No
If yes, who? _____
REACTION? _____

DRAW YOUR FART ⬅

OTHER NOTES: _____

FART

DATE: _____
TIME: _____
LOCATION: _____

Did it smell?
☐ Yes ☐ No

Smell-O-meter
(fill in the boxes)

not too bad ⟹ eye-watering

IF YES, CHECK ALL THAT APPLY
- ☐ cheesy
- ☐ beany
- ☐ eggy
- ☐ oniony
- ☐ malty
- ☐ musty
- ☐ nutty
- ☐ skunky
- ☐ sulfur
- ☐ spicy
- ☐ pungent
- ☐ earthy
- ☐ prune
- ☐ cabbage
- ☐ funk
- ☐ taco

DID YOU TAKE OWNERSHIP? ☐ Yes ☐ No
☐ Blamed dog

fill in to appropriate level

- ninja
- quack
- blast
- engine
- nuclear

NOISE LEVEL

Any witnesses?
☐ Yes ☐ No

IF YES, who? _____
REACTION? _____

DRAW YOUR FART ←

OTHER NOTES: _____

FART

DATE: _____
TIME: _____
LOCATION: _____

Did it smell?
☐ Yes ☐ No

IF YES, CHECK ALL THAT APPLY
- ☐ cheesy
- ☐ beany
- ☐ eggy
- ☐ oniony
- ☐ malty
- ☐ musty
- ☐ nutty
- ☐ skunky
- ☐ sulfur
- ☐ spicy
- ☐ pungent
- ☐ earthy
- ☐ prune
- ☐ cabbage
- ☐ funk
- ☐ taco

Smell-O-meter
(fill in the boxes)

not too bad ⟶ eye-watering

DID YOU TAKE OWNERSHIP? ☐ Yes ☐ No
☐ Blamed dog

fill in to appropriate level

- ninja
- quack
- blast
- engine
- nuclear

NOISE LEVEL

Any witnesses? ☐ Yes ☐ No
If YES, who? _____
REACTION? _____

DRAW YOUR FART ←

OTHER NOTES: _____

FART # ___

DATE: ___
TIME: ___
LOCATION: ___

Did it smell?
☐ Yes ☐ No

Smell-O-meter
(fill in the boxes)

not too bad ⟹ eye-watering

IF YES, CHECK ALL THAT APPLY
- ☐ cheesy
- ☐ beany
- ☐ eggy
- ☐ oniony
- ☐ malty
- ☐ musty
- ☐ nutty
- ☐ skunky
- ☐ sulfur
- ☐ spicy
- ☐ pungent
- ☐ earthy
- ☐ prune
- ☐ cabbage
- ☐ funk
- ☐ taco

DID YOU TAKE OWNERSHIP? ☐ Yes ☐ No ☐ Blamed dog

fill in to appropriate level

ninja | quack | blast | engine | nuclear

NOISE LEVEL

Any witnesses? ☐ Yes ☐ No
If YES, who? ___
REACTION? ___

DRAW YOUR FART ←

OTHER NOTES: ___

FART # ___

DATE: ___
TIME: ___
LOCATION: ___

Did it smell?
☐ Yes ☐ No

Smell-O-meter
(fill in the boxes)

not too bad ⟹ eye-watering

IF YES, CHECK ALL THAT APPLY
- ☐ cheesy
- ☐ beany
- ☐ eggy
- ☐ oniony
- ☐ malty
- ☐ musty
- ☐ nutty
- ☐ skunky
- ☐ sulfur
- ☐ spicy
- ☐ pungent
- ☐ earthy
- ☐ prune
- ☐ cabbage
- ☐ funk
- ☐ taco

DID YOU TAKE OWNERSHIP? ☐ Yes ☐ No ☐ Blamed dog

fill in to appropriate level

ninja | quack | blast | engine | nuclear

NOISE LEVEL

Any witnesses? ☐ Yes ☐ No
If YES, who? ___
REACTION? ___

DRAW YOUR FART ←

OTHER NOTES: ___

FART

DATE: _____
TIME: _____
LOCATION: _____

Did it smell?
☐ Yes ☐ No

Smell-O-meter
(fill in the boxes)

not too bad ⟹ eye-watering

IF YES, CHECK ALL THAT APPLY
- ☐ cheesy
- ☐ beany
- ☐ eggy
- ☐ oniony
- ☐ malty
- ☐ musty
- ☐ nutty
- ☐ skunky
- ☐ sulfur
- ☐ spicy
- ☐ pungent
- ☐ earthy
- ☐ prune
- ☐ cabbage
- ☐ funk
- ☐ taco

DID YOU TAKE OWNERSHIP?
☐ Yes ☐ No
☐ Blamed dog

NOISE LEVEL
fill in to appropriate level
- quack
- blast
- engine
- ninja
- nuclear

Any witnesses?
☐ Yes ☐ No

If yes, who? _____
REACTION? _____

DRAW YOUR FART ←

OTHER NOTES: _____

FART # ◯

DATE: _____
TIME: _____
LOCATION: _____

Did it smell?
☐ Yes ☐ No

IF YES, CHECK ALL THAT APPLY
- ☐ cheesy
- ☐ beany
- ☐ eggy
- ☐ oniony
- ☐ malty
- ☐ musty
- ☐ nutty
- ☐ skunky
- ☐ sulfur
- ☐ spicy
- ☐ pungent
- ☐ earthy
- ☐ prune
- ☐ cabbage
- ☐ funk
- ☐ taco

Smell-O-meter
(fill in the boxes)

not too bad ⟹ eye-watering

DID YOU TAKE OWNERSHIP? ☐ Yes ☐ No
☐ Blamed dog

fill in to appropriate level

- quack
- blast
- engine
- ninja
- nuclear

NOISE LEVEL

Any witnesses? ☐ Yes ☐ No

IF YES, who? _____
REACTION? _____

DRAW YOUR FART ←

OTHER NOTES: _____

FART

DATE: _____
TIME: _____
LOCATION: _____

Did it smell?
☐ Yes ☐ No

IF YES, CHECK ALL THAT APPLY
- ☐ cheesy
- ☐ beany
- ☐ eggy
- ☐ oniony
- ☐ malty
- ☐ musty
- ☐ nutty
- ☐ skunky
- ☐ sulfur
- ☐ spicy
- ☐ pungent
- ☐ earthy
- ☐ prune
- ☐ cabbage
- ☐ funk
- ☐ taco

Smell-O-meter
(fill in the boxes)

not too bad ➡ eye-watering

DID YOU TAKE OWNERSHIP? ☐ Yes ☐ No
☐ Blamed dog

fill in to appropriate level

- quack
- blast
- engine
- ninja
- nuclear

NOISE LEVEL

Any witnesses? ■ Yes ■ No
If YES, who? _____
REACTION? _____

DRAW YOUR FART ←

OTHER NOTES: _____

FART

DATE: _____
TIME: _____
LOCATION: _____

Did it smell?
☐ Yes ☐ No

IF YES, CHECK ALL THAT APPLY
- ☐ cheesy
- ☐ beany
- ☐ eggy
- ☐ oniony
- ☐ malty
- ☐ musty
- ☐ nutty
- ☐ skunky
- ☐ sulfur
- ☐ spicy
- ☐ pungent
- ☐ earthy
- ☐ prune
- ☐ cabbage
- ☐ funk
- ☐ taco

Smell-O-meter
(fill in the boxes)

not too bad ⟹ eye-watering

DID YOU TAKE OWNERSHIP? ☐ Yes ☐ No
☐ Blamed dog

NOISE LEVEL
fill in to appropriate level

- ninja
- quack
- blast
- engine
- nuclear

Any witnesses? ☐ Yes ☐ No

If YES, who? _____
REACTION? _____

DRAW YOUR FART ←

OTHER NOTES: _____

# FART #

DATE: _____
TIME: _____
LOCATION: _____

Did it smell?
☐ Yes ☐ No

Smell-O-meter
(fill in the boxes)

not too bad ⟶ eye-watering

IF YES, CHECK ALL THAT APPLY
- ☐ cheesy
- ☐ beany
- ☐ eggy
- ☐ oniony
- ☐ malty
- ☐ musty
- ☐ nutty
- ☐ skunky
- ☐ sulfur
- ☐ spicy
- ☐ pungent
- ☐ earthy
- ☐ prune
- ☐ cabbage
- ☐ funk
- ☐ taco

DID YOU TAKE OWNERSHIP? ☐ Yes ☐ No
☐ Blamed dog

NOISE LEVEL
fill in to appropriate level
- ninja
- quack
- blast
- engine
- nuclear

Any witnesses? ☐ Yes ☐ No
If yes, who? _____
REACTION? _____

DRAW YOUR FART ←

OTHER NOTES: _____

M.T. LOTT SAMPLE COLORING PAGES

from MONSTER FARTS COLORING BOOK

from SUPER CUTE FARTING ANIMALS COLORING BOOK

from THE FARTING MAGICAL CREATURES COLORING BOOK

from THE FORGOTTEN FAIRIES COLORING BOOK

from THE FARTING ANIMALS COLORING BOOK

Made in the USA
Monee, IL
05 December 2022